POEMS AND PRAYERS FROM THE HEART

By Craig Kiehl

Acts 17:28 For in him we live, and move, and have our being; as certain also of your own poets have said, For we are also his offspring.

Copyright © 2009 by Craig Kiehl

Poems and Prayers From The Heart
by Craig Kiehl

Printed in the United States of America

ISBN 978-1-60791-432-7

All rights reserved solely by the author. The author guarantees all contents are original and do not infringe upon the legal rights of any other person or work. No part of this book may be reproduced in any form without the permission of the author. The views expressed in this book are not necessarily those of the publisher.

Unless otherwise indicated, Bible quotations are taken from The KJV of the Bible. Copyright © 1979 by Christian Heritage Publishing.

Scriptures in Italic are words spoken by Jesus

www.xulonpress.com

CONTENTS

INTRODUCTION ix
   Poems And Prayers From The Heart............................ ix
   A Note To The Readers x
   The Crooked Tree xi
   God's Loving Mothers xiii

NEW LIFE IN CHRIST 17
   The Field Of Lights 18
   The Glory Of It All 19
   Hawaiian Island Paradise 21
   The Invitation 22
   It's Only By The Blood 23
   The Spirit Of God 24
   Where Will You Live 25
   God's Warehouse 26
   The Borrowed Tomb 28
   The One 29
   My King 31
   For You And Me 32
   Are You Sure You're Saved 34
   Driven By A Force 36
   Free 37
   Is This What You Think 38
   The Roads Of Life 40

v

Just Another Day 41
To Men And Women Of Honor...............................42
A Rainy Day...43
Heavenly Home 44
Temptation 45
The Importance Of Grace To Me 46

FAMILY AND FRIENDS 49
  To Family And Friends 50
  To Family And Friends On Thanksgiving Day............51
  My Gift From God 52
  To My Wife 54
  My Dearest Wife 55
  My Daughter The Traveling Vine 56
  Melissa And Judd 58
  Annabella And Grace 59
  My Special Son 60
  A Windy Day...62
  Merry Christmas To My Daughter Melissa 63
  Dear Whitney 64
  Christmas Time 65
  The Wonder Of Christmas 66
  The Forgotten Gift 67
  A Get Well Wish 68
  Happy Birthday Bob 69
  Home Coming Is A Special Time................................71
  Happy Birthday To My Mother-In-Law 73
  Father's Day...74
  A Father's Love..75
  Dad's Special Day..76
  To My Valentine..77
  Our Weekend...78
  Wedding On Butterfly Hill...79
  Give To Jerry Kids 80
  Happy 50th Anniversary..81

vi

Poems and Prayers From The Heart

PRAYERS 83
   A Prayer From The Heart 84
   Early Morning Prayer 85
   My Salvation 86
   Seeds Of Faith 87
   To My Loved Ones 88
   The Shipmaster 89
   A Revival Prayer 90
   The Lost 91
   Met A Women 93
   Few Months Ago 94
   A Parents Prayer 95
   Heavenly Insight 98

LIFE SORROWS 99
   Valleys Of Despair 100
   A Bad Day 102
   Divorce 103
   I Prayed To Our Lord 105
   Things To Remember 106
   In Memory Of Philomena Coy 107
   The Friend I Lost 108
   In Memory Of Brother Dugan 109

THE FINAL DAY 111
   A Dangerous World 112
   Jesus Is Coming 116
   What Do You Know 117
   Message From Above 118
   Terror In America 911 119
   Terror Continues 120
   A Cry For Peace 121
   The Final Day 122
   Talking About You—This Could Be You 123-124
   Decision Time 126

Introduction

Poems And Prayers From The Heart

I pray these poems and prayers may touch your heart and inspire you. These messages came to me by God's spirit. Some were written with many tears as I could feel God's presence as I wrote them. At times I felt such an urgency to record them I had to stop my car and write them down. I am truly humbled at God's presence in my life and at times felt drained and weak after receiving these. But as I praise him and thank him for each one, he renews my strength and fills me with joy. Some of these poems reflect my own life's experiences and others are inspired by people around me. But they all come from God above who sent his Son because of his love.

Psalms 126:5-6 They that sow in tears shall reap in joy. He that goeth forth and weepeth, bearing precious seed, shall doubtless come again with rejoicing, bringing his sheaves with him.

A Note To The Readers

The contents of this book are not bought or sold
There are things revealed in here the prophets of old longed
to know and behold

I may tell you things in here you may not believe
Things that only a spirit filled soul can receive

But I will tell you my hearts desire
That you would be filled with the Holy Ghost and fire

From his heart to mine, from mine to you
That you may know his love and forgiveness is for you

1st Corinthians 2:7-10 But we speak the wisdom of God in a mystery, even the hidden wisdom, which God ordained before the world unto our glory: Which none of the princes of this world knew: for had they known it, they would not have crucified the Lord of glory. But it is written, Eye hath not seen, nor ear heard, neither have entered into the heart of man, the things which God hath prepared for them that love him. But God hath revealed them unto us by his Spirit: for the Spirit searcheth all things, yea, the deep things of God.

1st Corinthians 2:12 Now we have received, not the spirit of the world, but the spirit which is of God; that we might know the things that are freely given to us of God.

It started with a prayer: **Jeremiah 33:3** Call unto me, and I will answer thee, and shew thee great and mighty things, which thou knowest not.

The Crooked Tree

I was driving to work which takes about a half hour. I often spend this time talking with the lord. I was thinking about all the struggles I was going through with my family, problems at work and finding a church that followed the leading of the Holy Spirit. I asked the Lord why is life so hard? He answered me just a few miles down the road with the crooked tree.

As I drove along the interstate there was a freshly excavated patch of land, on the edge of the opening there was a tree that appeared bent. Then I noticed it grew up about three feet then went horizontal for what appeared to be about 8 feet, then, its branches reached skyward. I thought about how the tree had grown in that condition. Had it been bent from the storms of life? Had it been overshadowed by larger trees? No matter what had happened the tree never gave up. It may be bent and crooked but it kept on reaching for the light. It had its roots in the good soil and knew if it kept reaching for the light all would be well, it could sprout leaves and bear fruit and spread its seeds. Then the Holy Spirit said to me, do the same no matter what happens, don't give up. Keep your feet planted in the good soil which is my word.

Keep reaching for the light which is my son. He said bear fruit and spread seeds tell everyone the great things I have done in your life. I then replied with this question. How is this going to happen? People don't listen to me. He said I will give you a voice that will be heard. As I continued driving to work with tears streaming down my face, I knew what I had to do. I needed to know God's word and how to present it, so people might be saved. I started filling myself with his word, studying and praying. I would take key scriptures and write them on a little scrap of paper, and pull it out of my pocket during the day to read and meditate on. Then I would also memorize them so I would have them when a need arose for myself or to share with others.

I remember the morning I wrote my first poem. As a child my mother told me to pick out a birthday card and write something nice inside it. I had all these cards spread out all over the table and they all said such nice things inside, but I could not think of a single word to write myself. I asked my mother how do they write such beautiful things? She told me that it comes from the heart. I wrote my first poem about 40 years later. I was sitting at my kitchen table and I picked up a pen and it flowed on to the paper without any struggling. I didn't even know I was going to do this. This poem is titled Gods Loving Mothers

God's Loving Mothers

A mother's love is always there
Her love is perfect, true and fair

She's on her knees each day in prayer
For she knows God's love and that he cares

The angels in heaven wait with open arms
To keep her children from all harm

Her prayers are felt from far away
For her love and Gods are here to stay

Psalms 91:10-12 There shall no evil befall thee, neither shall any plague come nigh thy dwelling. For he shall give his angels charge over thee, to keep thee in all thy ways.
    They shall bear thee up in their hands, lest thou dash thy foot against a stone.

I know that God orchestrates every area of our lives. We must keep our eyes and ears open to him. The Holy Spirit directed me to put **Psalms 91:10-12** at the bottom of this poem for my mother. When she read the poem for the first time she told me, no one knows this but when I pray every morning I claim this promise for all my children.

Mark 11:24 *Therefore I say unto you, What things soever ye desire, when ye pray, believe that ye receive them, and ye shall have them.*

As you continue to read this book I want you to expect to hear from God.

Luke 11:9-10 *And I say unto you, Ask, and it shall be given you; seek, and ye shall find; knock, and it shall be opened unto you. For every one that asketh receiveth; and he that seeketh findeth; and to him that knocketh it shall be opened.*

I started writing poetry in the year 2000. In late 2001 I decided I should write down my experienced with the crooked tree which I found very rewarding. The Holy Spirit told me at this time that this tree represented my life. I then asked, if this tree represents my life, why is it crawling along the ground? Why isn't it tall and strong like the cedars of Lebanon. I was told there is a limb on your tree that goes down to the earth, it has taken root and is sucking the life out of you. It is holding you down. When you cut if off you will be a vessel of honor fit for the Masters use. I wept, I knew what it was and it was holding me back from being the man God intended me to be.

I repented with many tears yet at times still had these same temptations. I have found that God loves me and understands. He is my Heavenly Father and I have been going through the process of becoming the person he has meant me to be from the foundation of the world.

I looked for the tree one day but could not find it anymore. I thought this fall when all the weeds die down I will be able to see my tree again. One morning I thought to look for the tree and there was a straight path through the brush and weeds, right where the tree had been. But it was gone. I thought somebody cut it down, it wasn't until later I realized this was God's way of showing me I was on the straight and narrow road, as John the Baptist said: make straight the way of the Lord which only comes through repentance.

In September of 2008 I graduated from Gateway of Hope Ministry School. School was challenging but so rewarding, the Holy Spirit molded us and shaped us into the image of the Lord Jesus Christ. The friendships I made with my brothers and sisters in Christ and the growth we experienced together will stand for eternity. The Lord has opened up a door and I want to be ready to step through it. The finishing of this book has been a strong desire of mine. I pray that it reaches into the inner most part of your soul and spirit.

From your faithful servant in Christ
Craig Kiehl

NEW LIFE IN CHRIST

II Corinthians 5:17 Therefore if any man be in Christ, he is a new creature: old things are passed away; behold, all things are become new.

The Field of Lights

There was a heavy frost on the grass as I walked my dog. I could hear and feel it crunching under my feet. It was then that I noticed the small yet bright sparkling lights scattered across the field. Every blade of grass that was turned in just the right direction caught and reflected the brightness from our security light. It was a beautiful sight to behold. They were like gems scattered all over, shinning in the darkness. As I moved around some of these lights went out and others appeared. Although it was cold I felt I could stand there forever admiring its beauty. It was such a large field I wished there were more lights. It was then that I sensed the awesome presence of God and heard from the spirit this message. I to wish there were more lights, this is what I see from Heaven, everyone, that has turned to me is a bright shinning light in the darkness of a world covered with sin. As my spirit moves across the earth calling the world to repent of their sins, I see new lights appearing as the people come to me. Some of the lights that go out are the saints of God that come home to be with me. But sadly others are those that lose their way and return to the darkness and a world of sin. There are some people lost in the darkness who have not heard about my son Jesus, who came and shed his blood that they could become as blades of grass catching and reflecting the perfect and pure image of my son the Light of the World. So let your light shine, stand in faith and be that bright and shinning light for those around you who are still in the dark.

Phiippians 2:15 That ye may be blameless and harmless the sons of God, without rebuke, in the midst of a crooked and perverse nation, among whom ye shine as lights in the world.

The Glory of It All

The morning air was crisp and fresh after the late night rain
Water trickled down the rocks as the hillsides drained

There were thin white clouds against a dark blue sky
Six birds in a formation came flying by

A rooster crowed announcing that morning had come
Then I saw a hillside now bright from the sun

On the hillside were cattle white, black and brown
They were all standing with their heads bowed down

The sound of birds singing filled the air
Two fawns frolicked in the field without a care

The wild flowers seemed to stand up so tall
There beauty and splendor surrounding it all

A tear rolled down my cheek after what I had seen
It was as if I had just walked into a dream

Everything was the way it was meant to be
It was put there for all to see

They all did what their creator meant them to do
God said to me then, how about you?

Genesis 1:26-28 And God said, Let us make man in our image, after our likeness: and let them have dominion over the fish of the sea, and over the fowl of the air, and over the cattle, and over all the earth, and over every creeping thing that creepeth upon the earth.

So God created man in his own image, in the image of God created he him; male and female created he them. And God blessed them, and God said unto them, Be fruitful, and multiply, and replenish the earth, and subdue it: and have dominion over the fish of the sea, and over the fowl of the air, and over every living thing that moveth upon the earth.

Hawaiian Island Paradise

The suns rays slowly revealed the wonders around
We heard the birds singing, the most beautiful sounds

We saw plants and flowers, lava rocks and trees
We saw marvelous sights and felt the ocean breeze

The majestic mountains with their cliffs reaching below
To the sand with the waves crashing in an endless flow

We saw waterfalls cascading high from above
Couples hand in hand renewing their love

People living out their dreams without any fears
Making friendships and memories that last through the years

On an island that was formed from the depths of the sea
By a God who created both you and me

A place that came about by words spoken from above
By our heavenly father who has sent us his love

A small dot in the ocean formed by the earths
inner most depths
By God's Son who we all need to receive and accept

John 1:3 All things were made by him; and without him was not anything made that was made.

The Invitation

It was sent out a long time ago
To reach you in time to save your soul

It was sent to us from Heaven above
It came from the Father because of his love

He knew that mankind had gone astray
So He sent his Son to show us the way

He built us a bridge that leads to streets of gold
With the most beautiful gardens you eyes could behold

The sky and the lakes are such a dark blue
The tree of life is there for me, for you

A place has been prepared for those who believe
Forgiveness of sin is freely received

The price has been paid by Jesus God's Son
For everything wrong you've ever done

You will have eternity with God when the trumpet sounds
In the Book of Life your name will be found

Revelation 3:5 *He that overcometh, the same shall be clothed in white raiment; and I will not blot out his name out of the book of life, but I will confess his name before my Father, and before his angels.*

Revelation 3:20 *Behold, I stand at the door, and knock: if any man hear my voice, and open the door, I will come in to him, and will sup with him, and he with me.*

It's Only By The Blood

It is at the cross, redemption came
As his blood spilled to the ground
The innocent blood, of the spotless lamb,
Was shed for those Hell bound

The hands that healed, nailed to the tree,
Bled for you and me
The feet that brought mankind good news
Were nailed to that tree

Those bloody stripes, laid on his back, he took in my place
Not just for me alone, but all the human race

From the crown of thorns, and when they pierced his side
Flowed the life giving blood, of the Savoir that died

The devil thought, that he had won
Killing Jesus, God's own Son

But! With his blood applied,
no ones denied entrance to his throne
The King of Kings says enter in to our Heavenly Home

Matthew 26:28 *For this is my blood of the new testament, which is shed for many for the remissions of sins.*

The Spirit Of God

God's spirit is moving across our land
Looking for people who will take a stand

People who will praise him with upraised hands
People who will share his life so grand

He is looking for people to let him in
So they can be set free from their sin

He is looking for people who will give up their pride
And walk with his spirit deep down inside

He's looking for hearts where he can reside
Hearts walking in his power helping others to decide

To receive the redeemer God's only Son
To receive forgiveness for all they have done

There's a place inside you only the gift of God can fill
So open your hearts and seek his will

John 14:15-20 *If ye love me, keep my commandments. And I will pray the Father, and he shall give you another Comforter, that he may abide with you for ever; Even the Spirit of truth whom the world cannot receive, because it seeth him not, neither knoweth him: but ye know him; for he dwelleth with you, and shall be in you. I will not leave you comfortless: I will come to you. Yet a little while, and the world seeth me no more; but ye see me; because I live, ye shall live also. At that day ye shall know that I am in my Father, and ye in me, and I in you.*

Where Will You Live

When Jesus was here he went from here to there
Telling people how much the Father cared

He had no dwelling to call his own
He slept in gardens or some ones home

He talked to his Father daily wherever he roamed
He had a direct line without a cell phone

He traveled all over but mostly he walked
The people came many miles to hear him talk

He told them things never heard before
He gave us a message we cannot ignore

He said Heaven and Earth will pass away
But if you come to me you'll have a place to stay

I've prepared you a mansion upon a hill
For all those that do my Fathers will

So come and receive what God has for you
He gave his only Son so you could live there too

John 14:1-3 *Let not your heart be troubled: ye believe in God, believe also in me. In my Father's house are many mansions: if it were not so, I would have told you. I go to prepare a place for you. And if I go and prepare a place for you, I will come again, and receive you unto myself; that where I am, there ye may be also.*

God's Warehouse

Come to God's Warehouse, his people are there
Their full of God's Love and know the Power of Prayer

You will find people there that will dare to believe
That God will give you what you need to receive

You will hear of God's Son and his Saving Grace
You will find your way out of this world's rat race

You will find the keys to the Kingdom that God freely gave
You will find Jesus who has the power to save

You will find Forgiveness for what you have done
When you receive Jesus, God's only Son

You will find Healing and Deliverance are freely given
For our Lord our Savior is Alive — HE HAS RISEN

There is Singing and Praying way beyond noon
And every ones hoping it will not end soon

It looks like any other warehouse on the out skirts of town
But that's where God's people with the Holy Ghost will be found

Mark 16:15-18 And he said unto them, *Go ye into all the world, and preach the gospel to every creature. He that believeth and is baptized shall be saved; but he that believeth not shall be damned. And these signs shall follow them that believe; In my name shall they cast out devils; they shall speak with new tongues; They shall take up serpents; and if* *they drink any deadly thing, it shall not hurt them, they shall lay hands on the sick, and they shall recover.*

The Borrowed Tomb

He came with a message that was food for the soul
Eyes and ears were opened, the lame were made whole

He is the first and the last, the beginning and the end
He is the gift of love that God did send

When he was born, they could not find a room
When he died he did not have a tomb

In a borrowed tomb our Lord's body did lay
No one knew then, that only three days he would stay

In three days he arose with the keys to hell, and the grave
He is risen he came to save

They came to the tomb looking for their Lord
You could tell by their tears he was loved and adored

He was seen by 500 before he left that last day
He's coming back for those who have found him
Jesus the only way

1st Corinthians 15:3-6 For I delivered unto you first of all that which I also received, how that Christ died for our sins according to the scriptures; And that he was buried, and that he rose again the third day according to the scriptures; And that he was seen of Cephas, then of the twelve; After that, he was seen of above five hundred brethren at once;

The One

I long to see my Saviors face
The one that saved me by his grace

The one that came to set me free
The one I call on bended knees

The one that came to make me whole
The one that came to clean my soul

The one that fills my heart within
The one that took away my sin

He carries all my guilt and shame
In my place he took the blame

For every thing that I have done
Jesus Christ, God's own Son

A crown of thorns placed on his head
Of the one that is the living bread

They nailed his hands and his feet
Of the one my soul longs to meet

The one they hung in agony
The one they nailed to a tree

The one that died at Calvary
So I might live eternally

Acts 4:12 Neither is there salvation in any other: for there is none other name under heaven given among men, whereby we must be saved.

My King

I walk each day with my King
Having a peace in my heart only he can bring

He's healed my heart my troubled soul
He's touched my life made me whole

He's healed my body many times before
His Love for me I cannot ignore

He spared my life when I went the wrong way
He sent his angels to hold me up on that day

He knows my thoughts my trouble, my fears
He answers my prayers that I've watered with tears

I know he speaks to you and to me
I hear his voice, he set me free

My faith in him continues to grow
It's his will I search with my heart to know

Psalm 23 1-6 The Lord is my shepherd; I shall not want. He maketh me to lie down in green pastures; he leadeth me beside the still waters. He restoreth my soul, he leadeth me in the paths of righteousness for his name's sake. Yea, though I walk through the valley of the shadow of death, I will fear no evil: for thou art with me; thy rod and thy staff they comfort me. Thou preparest a table before me in the presence of mine enemies: thou anointest my head with oil; my cup runneth over. Surely goodness and mercy shall follow me all the days of my life; and I will dwell in the house of the Lord for ever.

Poems and Prayers From The Heart

For You And Me

Jesus came for you and me
He died on the cross to set us free

He built a bridge to show us the way
It's there for you and me today

It's a bridge that takes us over troubled waters
It's there today for our sons and daughters

It isn't wide, it's very thin
But it covers a multitude of sin

It's a bridge that doesn't have a toll
When you cross it, you will be made whole

This bridge has a sign that says only one way
And Jesus is at the end every day

He's behind the door knocking; it's the door to your heart
When you let him in, you'll have a fresh start

It's the knocking you've heard all thru the years
When you come to him, he will take away your fears

He will comfort you, take away your sorrows
He will give you hope, of a better tomorrow

He's given, an invitation, to all not just some
His heart cry's for all to come

Matthew 7:13-14 *Enter ye in at the strait gate: for wide is the gate, and broad is the way, that leadeth to destruction,* *and many there be which go in thereat: Because strait is the gate, and narrow is the way, which leadeth unto life, and few there be that find it.*

Are You Sure You're Saved

Do you do his will every day of your life
Do you please him as you would as husband or wife

Do you think of him first when you wake up each day
Do you ask him to help you show others the way

Do you spend time learning what he came to earth to do
Do you know what he did for me and for you

What does he see when he looks down from above
Does he see an eternal soul that has received his love

Does he see a soul searching for earthly treasures
Or spiritual knowledge that comes with out measure

Are you so full of God's spirit that just your presence speaks loud
Or are you still a soul going along with the crowd

When people see you do they think of him
If so it's apparent you've been set free from sin

If you are full of the love that he freely gave
Then you should know in your heart that you are saved

Romans 10:13 For whosoever shall call upon the name of the Lord shall be saved.

1 John 5:11-13 And this is the record, that God hath given to us eternal life, and this life is in his Son. He that hath the Son hath life; and he that hath not the Son of God hath not life. These things have I written unto you that believe on the name of the Son of God; that ye may know that ye have eternal life, and that ye may believe on the name of the Son of God.

Driven By A Force

For 25 years I was driven by a force
I thought I was in control I did not know its source

I was young and ambitious and full of pride
I didn't understand who was at my side

His influence on me I did not see
I did not know what he would do to me

He stole my wife and my self esteem
He broke my heart and took away my dreams

I said to myself I need a change
Then I met a man who seemed a little strange

He told me things that helped me understand
He told me about God and his plan

He told me about Satan the great Deceiver
He told me about Jesus and I became a believer

Now I'm driven by God's spirit
I'm ready to share it with all that will hear it

1 Peter 5:6-8 Humble yourselves therefore under the mighty hand of God, that he may exalt you in due time: Casting all you care upon him; for he careth for you. Be sober, be vigilant; because your adversary the devil, as a roaring lion, walketh about, seeking whom he may devour:

Free

Can you say free now free now free at last
Free from all the sins of my past

Free from all the sins you've done
Covered by the Blood of Jesus God's Son

Never to be remembered ever again
May his kingdom come, the kingdom without end

Romans 8:2 The law of the Spirit of life in Christ Jesus hath made me free from the law of sin and death.

John 8:36 *If the Son therefore shall make you free, ye shall be free indeed.*

Is This What You Think

I'd like to go to church but I've been bad
When I think of what I've done I get sad

I don't want my sins coming to the light
So I try to hide them from his sight

But my sins haunt me every night
I'm drawn to them without a fight

Oh what an evil person am I
There seems to be nothing left but to die

But Jesus knows all of your fears
He says come to me I'll dry your tears

Confess your sins, I will forgive
I will dwell in you, you will start to live

Read my word it's powerful and true
I will show you what you need to do

I will clean you up I will cleanse your soul
I will give you hope which Satan has stole

This is a promise from our Lord
In the Bible his promises are stored

1st John 1:8-10 If we say that we have no sin, we deceive ourselves, and the truth is not in us. If we confess our sins, he is faithful and just to forgive us our sins, and to cleanse us from all unrighteousness. If we say that we have not sinned, we make him a liar, and his word is not in us.

2nd Timothy 3:16-17 All scripture is given by inspiration of God, and is profitable for doctrine, for reproof, for correction, for instruction in righteousness: That the man of God may be perfect, thoroughly furnished unto all good works.

The Roads Of Life

I think of where I could have been
Suffering under a load of sin

The sins in my life we're such a heavy load
They stuck to me like glue takes hold

I look back at my life and what I have done
I used to think I was having such fun

I was on a road that seemed to have no end
I was lonely and without a friend

Then I found a road that said only one way
I found there were rest stops for every day

The road is narrow but smooth you will not stumble
Just open your heart and make yourself humble

This road is never in need of repair
Jesus, God's Son is always there

Matthew 7:13-14 *Enter ye in at the strait gate: for wide is the gate, and broad is the way, that leadeth to destruction, and many there be which go in thereat: Because strait is the gate, and narrow is the way, which leadeth unto life, and few there be that find* it.

Just Another Day

It's another day to work and play
It's another day to watch what you say

The words of your mouth are powerful for sure
They could start a fire or help others endure

My words have caused problems in my life
They have caused me plenty of strife

My pride has gotten me in some trouble
But God humbled me busting my bubble

Now he's in my heart speaking to me
He's teaching me, allowing me to see

He's showing me his forgiveness and his love
He's giving me understanding that comes from above

Now I'm trying to listen to his voice
I'm trying to make just the right choice

I'm looking to him for the right words to say
For he's showed me, it's not just another day

James 3: 10 Out of the same mouth proceedeth blessing and cursing. My brethren, these things ought not so to be.

James 3:13 Who is a wise man and endued with knowledge among you? Let him shew out of a good conversation his works with meekness of wisdom.

To Men And Women Of Honor

They look like ordinary men and women you see around town
But when faced with challenges they stand there ground

They are dedicated, unselfish always helping others
I am proud to call them my sister and brother

Their minds are focused their job is to serve
They do more for us than we could ever deserve

They take pride in finishing everything they start
They are good and honest, pure in heart

They choose to serve others, not their own will
They stand for justice and oppose evil

They're men and women of valor that give their all
They leave homes and family to answer this call

They leave us and go places we would not dare
They are full of courage, they go anywhere

I embrace each one as they serve us each day
I want to remind them God's help is just a prayer away

Psalms 31:14-16 But I trusted in thee, O Lord: I said, Thou art my God. My times are in thy hand: deliver me from the hand of mine enemies, and from them that persecute me. Make thy face to shine upon thy servant; save me for thy mercies sake.

A Rainy Day

A rainy day can slow you down
It can change your plans or make you frown

It's a day to do things you may have let go
Like clean the house or go to a show

A rainy day can be a welcome retreat
If you worked hard all through the week

It can be a time to reflect on days gone by
It can be a time to laugh, pray or cry

It can be a time to be alone, go see others
Or take a nap under the covers

But most of all it's another day God gave
To praise him, for he came to save

Psalms 145:3 Great is the Lord, and greatly to be praised; and his greatness is unsearchable.

Heavenly Home

I long to see his streets of gold
And every thing his eyes behold

The gardens and the dark blue sky
The mansions made for you and I

I long to see his pearly gates
To walk through them I'll have to wait

And at the supper of the Lamb
I'll sit and eat with the great I am

I long to hear him say well done
Enter in my precious son

I'll thank him for the battles won
By faith in Jesus, God's own Son

I'll throw my crown at his feet
When my Savior I shall meet

I give him all the praise he's due
The one that made my soul brand new

II Corinthians 5:1 For we know that if our earthly house of this tabernacle were dissolved, we have a building of God, an house not made with hands, eternal in the heavens.

Temptation

When temptation came knocking at my door
I should have dropped to my knees on the floor

Instead I turned the knob and I invited him in
It was then I revisited the same old sin

The spirit said stop to my flesh and bones
Now the devil accuses me while throwing stones

I know I've denied my precious Lord
The one I claimed to have loved and adored

I am so mad at myself that I chose the wrong way
So I got on my knees and began to pray

With bitter tears, I began to repent
That I might hear from the spirit that he has sent

Through my weakness, he has made me strong
Next time the devil comes knocking I will choose right not wrong

James 1:12 Blessed is the man that endureth temptation: for when he is tried, he shall receive the crown of life, which the Lord hath promised to them that love him.

THE IMPORTANCE OF GRACE TO ME

God's Grace came to me in a time of my life when I was living in deep despair
and loneliness. I had worked four different jobs, lived in four different apartments. My child was diagnosed with severe learning disabilities and my wife and I divorced all in about a 4 year period.

I started understanding God's Grace as free the night I was given a Bible the
Good News for Modern Man. I started reading the word of God. I knew there had to be something that would help me. I was asked a question that night after the Bible study. What do you think? I said I don't know what you have but I want it, and that night I got it GRACE.

Ephesians: 2:8 For by grace are ye saved through faith; and that not of yourselves: it is a gift of God:

Reading the word of God had stirred something inside of me that I did not fully understand but it is that night that I received peace inside. I knew something different was happening to me. I knew it was a spiritual awakening. I had been given this precious book which holds God's thoughts, his purpose, and his plan and reveals his love. His provision of Grace is revealed to mankind by the Holy Spirit. Not bought or sold but applied through faith to every believer in Jesus Christ. That night I was seeking and I felt and knew Christ and the Grace he has provided.

Grace released me from the debt I owed for all the things I ever did wrong. I felt like I just received the Get out of Jail Free Card for my life. I had already decided to make a change in my life. But now I felt renewed like I had not known since I was a child.

Grace brought me joy and it was very evident. I wanted to tell everyone. The change was so evident that people thought I was mixed up in a cult. I learned that Grace made me acceptable in the sight of God even though I did nothing to deserve it.

Now that I am acceptable to him by Grace it opens the door of communication with him. I can now make my petitions known to him which exhibits my Faith that he is my provider.

Walking in Grace has empowered me to hear by the Holy Spirit the word of God with understanding which shapes and molds me into his likeness that I might do the things he has intended for me to do.

Grace gives me victory in every area of my life; it preserves my soul for eternity. Grace is applied daily as I walk on this earth. I am growing in Grace each day.

Grace releases me from the bondage of sin, and also gives me full pardon which, frees me from the guilt in my conscience of the past. Grace tears down the wall conceived in my heart and mind that separates me from God.

Grace transformed me into the man I am today. I am seeking to do his will in every area of my life and share Grace to those that do not know the victory in Gods Grace.

The most important thing I have learned about Grace is that it is renewed day by day. With Grace applied your not denied any of God's blessings. Jesus told Nicodemus that which is born of the flesh is flesh and that which is born of the spirit is spirit. When you are born of the flesh, which we all were, we needed to be nurtured by our parents. They fed us, clothed us, they loved us and there is nothing they would not do for us. The first years of our life they cleaned us up. It was a daily event you know, those dirty diapers.

When you are born again which is a spiritual birth you receive Grace upon Grace which is the fullness of Christ. **John 1:16**

As you start walking in your new life in the spirit you find yourself being transformed into a new person.
II Corinthians 5:17 If any man be in Christ he is a new person. Old things are past away and all things become new.

The spirit of Grace feeds our souls, cloths us with righteousness. Grace shows us love and affection which grows into graciousness in us and when Grace is first applied in our lives there is a lot of cleaning up to do. Remember the dirty laundry?

I thank God for Grace given to us by our Heavenly Father through Jesus Christ the Lord of our lives.

Grace Not Known

Grace not known such victory lost
By our friends and our family that know not the cost
Paid once for all, Grace freely given
The price has been paid by the one that is Risen
A secret revealed his story now told
Grace is full pardon not earned bought or sold

FAMILY AND FRIENDS

Poems and Prayers From The Heart

To Family And Friends

I think of you often, I love you and care
I bring your names before the Lord in humble prayer

Lord, keep them all in the best of health
Give them your knowledge which is better than wealth

Help them to understand what Jesus has done
Show them the love of God's only Son

Show them lord what life is all about
So they would call on your Son, having no doubts

That Jesus is in charge, he runs the show
And when the trumpet sounds all those that believe will go

Poems and Prayers From The Heart

I wrote this poem about our daughter. When I think of her I think about the vine traveling along a rock wall searching for and exploring life. My wife and I are the sun and the rain and the buds that opened are the wonderful things we saw her accomplish. The end of the wall is when she left home then as parents we started praying even more. The rainbow is a sign of Gods beautiful promises to us as believers.

When you walk in Gods promises your life is in full bloom and you will have love to give to others. This poem was in my notebook for a number of years unfinished. I would read it and did not have the words in my heart to finish it. I have learned to have patience and let God work in my life. I wrote the last five lines for this poem after our daughter gave birth to twins, Annabella Rose and Grace Katherine. As you read **Revelation 4:2-3** you will see why I said there is no end to a rainbow.

Revelation 4:2-3 And immediately I was in the spirit, and, behold, a throne was set in heaven, and one sat on the throne. And he that sat was to look upon like a jasper and a sardine stone: and there was a rainbow round about the throne, in sight like unto an emerald

My Daughter the Traveling Vine

The vine started growing along our rock wall
It grew to the top and started to crawl

The sun and the rain nourished it for awhile
The vine grew buds that opened and caused us to smile

Sometimes the vine left the wall and grew out where we drive
So we would stop and move it so it would survive

My Dearest Wife

It was twenty years ago you entered my life
The day God made us one in his sight

I remember the day I prayed for someone special in my life
It was the very same day the Lord told me you would be my wife

I saw you worshiping, eyes closed, your hands reaching above
I felt something stir in my heart I knew it was love

I could not see you each day, it was not my choice
So I called you each day just to hear your voice

The times we were apart I almost couldn't bear
I knew God had answered my prayer

If the Lord had made me wait these twenty years of my life
And I met you today I would ask you to be my wife

To My Wife
The love of my life

Who can light up my day?
By only looking my way

Your love exceeds
My wants and my needs

Your compassion and care
You're willing to share

And when put to the test
You're always the best

She's my faithful companion
Whom I'll never abandon

Next to God she's the love of my life
She is my gift from God, she is my wife

My Gift from God

It was 18 years ago on Mother's Day
My son and I sat down to pray

I said Lord please give us a mother and a wife
Someone special to share our life

The first time I saw her she had upraised hands
God told me then about his plans

He said this is the wife I give to thee
I said Lord are you sure, she'll never have me

But our paths crossed again that very same day
She and I talked while our children played

I started phoning her almost every day
It seemed we always had plenty to say

The times we were apart I almost couldn't bear
Because I knew God had answered my prayer

Her voice is so sweet, her smile so pleasant
She's my gift from God, a wonderful present

She can light up my day
By only looking my way

Her compassion and care
She's always willing to share

Her love and devotion
Fills me with emotion

To Family and Friends
On Thanksgiving Day
May your day be full of Love and God's Blessings

It's a time to look back at days gone by
Months seem like days, time really flies

It's a day to be with family and friends
Giving thanks no matter what life may send

It's a day to look back at what's taken place
It's a time to remember a loved ones face

I think about this year and what I've done
Sometimes were hard, but others were fun

This year has had some tragedy and fears
I hear of lives lost it brings me to tears

I pray to my savior for a special touch
By faith I know I'm not asking too much

He gives me strength and the desire to care
He causes me to love and want to share

So I give thanks today to God above
No matter what happens I still feel his love

We watched the vine travel to the end of the wall
It had no where to go but to stop or fall

So we looked to the heavens to God above
We found a rainbow he sent full of love

Now this tender vine is traveling on a rainbow with no end
Her life's in full bloom with so much love to send

Now she has two vines growing along her own rock wall
She will be very busy when they start to crawl

She will have to look to the heavens to God above
To lead them to that rainbow God sent full of love

There is no end to a rainbow

Melissa And Judd

The Birth of a child by two joined in love
Is a blessing from our Father Above

God poured out a Blessing on both of you
Instead of one he gave you two

To love them and guide them and show them the way
You will need God's help everyday

God never gives us more than we can do
That's why he blessed you with not one but two

Annabella And Grace

The two of you arrived just a year ago
We've looked on in amazement as we watched you grow

Sometimes you cry, we wonder what is wrong
So we hold you close and sing you a song

Your laughs, your smiles, your cute little giggles
The way you jump up and down your cute little wiggles

We watched you find your fingers and toes
As you played with each other touching your ears and nose

Your eyes take in everything new in sight
Sometimes you pull on the same toy with all your might

To watch your first few steps and hear the way you chatter
There's nothing else in our hearts that seems to matter

My Special Son

I have a son who's stuck between a child and a man
I sometimes wondered about God's plan

The first years of his life were full of unrest
We asked all the Doctors they all did their best

Special Education and Residential Treatment they say
The next thing I knew they had taken him away

He was moved out of my home for ten long years
I'd go visit him there and drive home with tears

At the age of twenty-one they moved him to a farm
They said he will be safe there, free from harm

He wasn't there more than a few days
When he told me on his birthday he was running away

He and a man shared an eight by ten room
They took care of the cows and were all done by noon

The rest of the day they had nothing to do
Once a week they walked to town a mile or two

They all took turns cooking and cleaning
They rest of the day was spent day dreaming

So I brought him home and tried my best
I prayed to God that he'd do the rest

At times he has so much love to give
He's showed me God's love and how to forgive

He depends on me and wants my time and love
Just as I need help from my Father above

A Windy Day

It was a windy day the sun was bright
It was a wonderful day to fly a kite

So my son and I went out to play
We watched the kite go up, up and away

The kite went up fast the sun was so bright
Neither of us could see our soaring kite

My son was sure I had lost his kite
Because it wasn't within his site

So I gave him the string, he began to smile
He could feel it pulling up there almost a mile

Now I think of Jesus whom I cannot see
Yet I feel him so close, right next to me

I feel a constant pull that is always there
I know his love, I know he cares

When he came to earth, he had something to do
He gave his life, for me and for you

He knew of things, we could not see
One day he will show them to you and me

Merry Christmas
To My Daughter Melissa

I'll be thinking of you on Christmas
Wishing you were here

I hope your day is full of love
That takes away your fears

It's a day we look to God above
And receive his peace and joy

It's the day God sent to earth
A special little boy

We celebrate his perfect birth
He came for you and me

So he could show us the only way
That heaven we may see

Dear Whitney

I heard about your Christmas wish
So I sent this card to you

I said a prayer for you today
And your family too

I searched for the right words to say
To help you through the day

I know that God is there with you
Every step of the way

My heart has opened up to you
I think of you each day

I'll mention you in my daily prayers
For I know God loves you and he really cares

May God strengthen you!
And hold you up even in your darkest hours

Christmas Time

I'll be thinking of you on Christmas
It's a day of peace and joy

Giving gifts of perfect love
To little girls and boys

God sent his Son down to earth
To share him with you

So you could know his perfect love
And share his birthday too

The Wonder of Christmas

The bright lights sparkled on the snow and ice
I gazed out the window it looks so nice

Everyone's preparing for Christmas Eve
It's a time of giving, a time to receive

It's not all lights and Santa Clause
It's about a baby who came with a cause

God gave his son to Joseph and Mary
For to Bethlehem he had to be carried

To fulfill the scriptures it had to be done
Concerning the birth of God's only Son

When they arrived there was no room at the inn
Where would this precious child's life begin?

Joseph and Mary found a manger
It was there he was born out of danger

God placed a star in the eastern sky
He sent his angels to tell the Shepard's why

They came and worshipped the new born king
They left praising God with a new song to sing

Now God's Son grew up to show us the way
I invited him in my heart he's there today

So accept the gift that God freely gave
For he alone has the power to save

The Forgotten Gift

On a clear crisp morning around mid December
I wrapped Christmas presents and tried to remember

Was there another present I needed to get?
Was there someone else I didn't want to forget?

I looked out the frosted window at the morning sun
I thought to myself will I ever get done

I cut and I wrapped for what seemed like a year
Where is the peace and joy, I used to hold so dear

Then I remembered the gift given to me
He changed my life and set me free

He's the reason I celebrate Christmas each year
He fills me with love, peace and joy, he takes away fears

He came to give hope he was sinless from birth
For the gift of God has come down to earth

A Get Well Wish

I heard of a poem that was sent from up North
It took ten minds to bring it forth

They tried to write what was on their mind
They searched and searched for what they could find

They had the nerve to send it in the mail
Though they walked right past the garbage pail

I received a call telling me what they had done
So I could choose to open it or run

When it finally arrived I opened it with fear
But their love and concern was very clear

It was nice they would try to write down their thoughts
When a get well card they could have bought

I thank you all for doing your best
When it comes to poems I'll write the rest

Happy Birthday Bob

This poem was written in 2001, 22 years after I met Bob. My sister was visiting him all the time and many people were praying for him. This same group of people had been praying for me also.

I received Gods love and forgiveness in September 1978 and in January 1979 I was baptized and filled with the Holy Spirit. My family noticed the radical change in my life, but on the flip side did not fully understand the change in me. My sister asked me to go see Bob, and tell him about the changes in my life. At the time he spent most of his time bedridden or on crutches. He had a disease called hemophilia. The average life span of a person having hemophilia was about 30 years. This is a crippling blood disorder that causes you to bleed internally, especially at your joints and also organs like your kidneys. What happened next is what I have grown to recognize as the leading of the Holy Spirit. I told him that he needed to stop doing anything that was displeasing to God. Then he should go to a church where the Holy Spirit was allowed to move and God would raise him up.

I received a call one night from my sister, telling me that they had gone to a church service in another town. Bob went to the alter on his crutches for prayer. He had one leg that was always bent at the knee and was unable to straighten it. When they prayed for him, his leg straightened out. Praise God he started walking again with a limp, but he had started down the road of faith. Bob and Laurie were married and he worked for awhile repairing furniture. Then the Lord led him to Bible school and now he is the Pastor of a Church. Now his work is leading souls to Christ instead of repairing furniture he is repairing lives. I want to tell you to get on the path God has for you and he will take you through.

Happy Birthday Bob

When I met you I was told there wasn't a chance
That you'd get out of that bed, walk or dance

Doctor's said you had lived over half of your life
You'd never have children or a wife

You would never work or drive a car
You would never travel very far

You would never do what other people can
But they didn't know about God's plan

He raised you up and set your goals
Even when health tried to take its toll

You are a miracle of God for all to see
One day I will see you come running at me

Jumping and shouting on streets of Gold
Singing praises to God with the saints of old

James 5:14-15 Is any sick among you? Let him call for the elders of the church; and let them pray over him, anointing him with oil in the name of the Lord: And the prayer for faith shall save the sick, and the Lord shall raise him up, and if he have committed sins, they shall be forgiven him.

Home Coming Is A Special Time

It's a time to visit with sisters and brothers
Friends and neighbors, fathers and mothers

It's a time to look at what's taken place
A time to remember a loved ones face

It's a time to catch up on days gone by
Things that make us laugh, things that make us cry

It's a time to come together with people that care
People you can count on to always share

It's a place I know I can count on others
A place where everyone loves one another

A place I can share my joy and sorrows
A place of faith of an endless tomorrow

A place full of memories of things from the past
Good times and bad things that make us laugh

Smiling faces of the young and old
Memories only our hearts can hold

It's a place that is always steadfast and sure
A place that we feel safe and secure

I think of Sister Malone's prayers that reach God's throne
Healings taking place in heart, mind and bone

Tear stained faces that pray through the night
Saints of God who know things will be all right

A place we share times with loved ones and friends
A place we long to go no matter what life may send

I think of Granny Bane's banana pudding, ice cream and apple pies
Days spent picnicking under the clear blue sky

Children running up and down the isle with great big smiles
A place I'd travel to if it was a thousand miles

Some day we will travel to our heavenly home far away
I know in my heart we will rejoice in that day

For he has prepared a place with streets of Gold
With the most beautiful gardens your eyes can behold

I envision the sky and the lakes being such a dark blue
And the tree of life is there for me and for you

At the marriage supper of the Lamb, when were with God's Son
Giving him thanks for all he has done

We will have eternity with God when the trumpet sounds
Because in the Book of Life our names will be found

This is a promise from our Lord and in the Bible his promises are stored

Happy Birthday To My Mother-In-Law

To a mother - in - law who's a pleasure to be around
She has some of the best daughters to be found

She is lots of fun, she always cares
She's full of love, always willing to share

She is always thinking of others before herself
If she was a wine she would be top shelf

Father's Day

A Father is special like a sunny day
He's there to guide you and show you the way

He's there to teach you and help you to learn
He's full of love and shows his concern

His example of love has a lasting effect
It makes us want to show our respect

He has given me everything that he could
He always does what a good father should

I long to talk with him every day
I have lots of things I'd like to say

To thank him for always being there
For always listening, I know he cares

So I remember him on this special day
For he's in my heart what more can I say

Proverbs 4:1-4 Hear, ye children, the instruction of a father, and attend to know understanding. For I give you good doctrine, forsake ye not my law. For I was my Father's Son, tender and only beloved in the sight of my mother. He taught me also, and said unto me, Let thine heart retain my words: keep my commandments, and live.

A Father's Love

There's a place in a Father down deep inside
A place where his deepest thoughts reside

A place of concern for those that he loves
It's what he stands for and what he does

It's what he works for every day of his life
Stability, a provider for children and wife

A Father who knows his strength comes from above
Is a Father who prays and knows God's love

He thinks of his family no matter what the cost
He pays the price that they may not be lost

Dad's Special Day

A Dad's birthday is such a special day
It's so hard to find the right words to say

He's firm and stern but he really cares
He's full of love and he always shares

You can always tell when Dad is mad
But when you do well he's proud and glad

The world is full of trouble and fears
But dad has advice and knowledge of many years

I thank you Dad for always being there
I love you dad and I really care

To My Valentine

I wish I had money to send you flowers
Every minute we're apart seems like hours

I have to leave you each day, I have no choice
Some days I call you just to hear your voice

When you smile your face is aglow with love
It's as if God sent an angel down from above

Your faithfulness to me makes me feel so secure
For your love and God's are the same for sure

You are always concerned and you always care
You're full of God's love and willing to share

Showering you with gifts I would love to do
But today all I have to give is my love to you

Our Weekend

I looked forward to this weekend
To spend time with both of you

We live so very far apart
So these two days will have to do

The weather was perfect and our fellowship divine
It would have been perfect even if the sun did not shine

We shared this time and built memories
That will last thru out the years

Our hearts have joined together
We feel a closeness that will endure

Love is planted deep within our hearts
This time was dear for sure

Wedding On Butterfly Hill

There is something fluttering on Butterfly Hill
It started in the hearts of Glenn and Cheryl

They had a dream of a home facing the setting sun
A labor of love that is finally done

Now the two of them become one, facing the western sky
Watching the setting sun and the Butterflies

I received a call from my sister Sherry, who lives in Florida and works for the MDA. A group of employees she works with were raising money. She told me about the name they chose for their team and what the money would be used for, helping boys and girls with this disease. They were using Green and Gold shamrocks which were posted all over the walls in stores when people donated. The Green shamrocks were used for $1.00 donations and the Gold for larger donations. I hope you enjoy reading this poem as much as I enjoyed writing it.

Give to Jerry's Kids

There are green and gold shamrocks all over town
That's where St. Petersburg pirates will be found

Asking you to help a boy or girl today
It's only a dollar what do you say?

We are counting on you all to give and to share
Show how much you really love and care

Summer camps, support groups and a clinic
Your dollars are needed this is no gimmick

Money for research to find a cure
A child's life may change for sure

St. Petersburg Pirates will not be out sold
When you give to M.D.A. go for the gold

Happy 50th Anniversary

It's been fifty years since you became husband and wife
The day you became one in God's sight

You took a vow that you knew was for life
It's taken you through differences that turned out all right

You showed us love beyond compare
You're always willing to give and to share

Your lives show us commitment that is full of faithfulness
And when things went wrong there was always forgiveness

You have showed us a bond that will not let go
When we needed you, there was always a hand to hold

All these things that are written in these lines above
You both gave to us, because of your love

Genesis 2:24 Therefore shall a man leave his father and his mother, and shall cleave unto his wife: and they shall be one flesh.

PRAYERS

1 Peter 3:12 For the eyes of the Lord are over the righteous, and his ears are open unto their prayers: but the face of the Lord is against them that do evil.

John 15:7 *If ye abide in me, and my words abide in you, ye shall ask what ye will, and it shall be done unto you.*

Psalm 91:15 He shall call upon me, and I will answer him: I will be with him in trouble, I will deliver him, and honour him.

A Prayer from the Heart

A Prayer from the heart of those filled with his love
Reach the Throne room of God in the heavens above

He stores them like treasures, so I have been told
To him they are more precious than silver or gold

He sends out the answer to each and everyone
Every prayer that is prayed in the name of his Son

I tell you the heavens are moved and the earth below
By the prayers of his son and the seeds that they sow

John 14:13-14 *What so ever you ask the Father in my name that shall I do that the Father may be glorified in the Son, if you shall ask anything in my name I will do it.*

Early Morning Prayer

I prayed to our Lord for the right words say
For his help and protection through out the day

I prayed that I would be a blessing to others
Even people that are not Christian brothers

I prayed for forgiveness for things that I've done
I prayed to the Father in the name of his Son

I thanked him for the blessing he's done in my life
For my sons and daughter and my lovely wife

I thanked him for the knowledge of his word
And every great truth I've ever heard

I thanked him for giving us his only Son
That's something I don't think I could possibly have done

The love and concern he has shown to us all
That we may all be his family that answer his call

Psalms 5:3 My voice shalt thou hear in the morning, O Lord; in the morning will I direct my prayer unto thee, and will look up.

My Salvation

My salvation is what I want to share
Showing people that they need to care

I gave Jesus my heart and I cry within
Lord please forgive me of my sin

Help me to walk in your love and power
Keep me doing your will each and every hour

Let my life shine and show you to others
So that someday I may call them all brothers

Lord work in my life everyday
Please give me the right words to say

To lead the lost to your door
So they fall to their knees on the floor

Broken hearted looking for you
For nothing but your perfect love will do

Lord, pour out your blessing all over me
So my precious Jesus they may see

John 1:4 In him was life; and the life was the light of men.

Seeds of Faith

Through seeds of Faith from a single prayer
To the Father above to the one that cares

The Heavens are moved and the earth below
By the saints of God the Lord Jesus knows

His promises held by those that believe
By those that love him by those who receive

From the Spirit of truth who sends what we need
Of the knowledge of him that their souls might be freed

Hebrews 11:1 Now faith is the substance of things hoped for, the evidence of things not seen.

To My Loved Ones

I have lots of things I'd like to share
I think of you often, I love you and care

My belief in God is one of those
But what you believe, God only knows

I pray for you each and every day
That you would open your ears to what God has to say

My joy and peace come from above
God sent his Son to show us his love

He gave us his word which is powerful and true
That you may have life and have it brand new

To experience the healing from God's only Son
Just ask him in your heart the battles been won

With tears of joy he'll accept you in
And a wonderful life you will begin

You'll have eternity with God when the trumpet sounds
Because in the book of life your name will be found

The Shipmaster

I set sail at the first sign of day break
My ship moved the calm waters as I headed for the lake

I watched each wave I caused head for the shore
I wondered what this day had in store

A strong wind blew as I entered the lake
It moved the waters causing white caps to break

I felt each wave as it hit the ships side
I steadied my feet waiting for each one to collide

The spray of water was on my face
I could feel my anxiety starting to race

I fought the ships wheel as I ponder my fate
I called out to Jesus before it was too late

Suddenly the fear in my heart fled away
As I realized his presence is with me every step of the way

Proverbs 3:5-6 Trust in the Lord with all thine heart: and lean not unto thine own understanding. In all they ways acknowledge him, and he shall direct thy paths.

A Revival Prayer

There's been prayer for revival all through the week
To our Lord we look, with our hearts we seek

With anticipation of what God wants to do
Will he do it for me, will he do it for you

With love and concern we pray to our Lord
For people to receive the gifts he has stored

We pray for the presence of the Holy Spirit
We pray that the lost will come and hear it

For the sick and the lonely, and those full of hate
That they would find Jesus before its too late

That knowledge and wisdom be given to our Pastor
That our hearts would be filled with joy and laughter

That we would be filled with the Holy Ghost and fire
That God's will, would be our hearts desire

We pray our church would be a place to find God's Son
To find forgiveness for what they have done

For Jesus has come to show us the way
He's listening for your voice every day

Come and receive what god has for you
For there is nothing, no nothing he cannot do

The Lost

There are many people I see each day
I know they are lost by what they say

They lie and gossip and even swear
They do what they want, they don't seem to care

They act this way, they have no fear
God's truth, his word, they do not hear

Many will say you should not judge
Give them God's word, they still won't budge

Let me tell you who, these people are
You won't have to look very far

They're beside you behind you and even above
They may be someone you really love

Now Jesus came to save the lost
He paid with his life the ultimate cost

He had friends and family just like you
But the will of the Father he had to do

He prayed to the Father, but it had to be done
The Father sacrificed his only Son

He defeated Satan, the great deceiver
So you and I could become a believer

Now he's filled us with the Holy Spirit
So we can share God's love to all that will hear it

So if the spirit of God shows you someone is lost
Try to reach them, no matter the cost

Isaiah 61:1 The spirit of the Lord God is upon me; because the Lord hath anointed me to preach good tidings unto the meek; he hath sent me to bind up the brokenhearted, to proclaim liberty to the captives, and the opening of the prison to them that are bound.

I met a women one morning while buying coffee. The next day I was led by the Holy Spirit to pray for her needs. That is when I wrote this poem, Met a Women. During the next few months our paths crossed again at the coffee shop and one day in the hospital where my son was having surgery. We knew each other by sight, I did not know her name and she didn't know mine. But we had shared our family concerns with each other. The last time I saw her was in a parking lot her baby was close to a year old. The baby kept reaching for me wanting to come to me, as I held her child she said I cannot believe it. She never goes to men. I wasn't surprised just blessed of God.

Met A Women

I met a woman the other day
She talked of her problems, she had plenty to say

Her husband faced a layoff, they had bills to pay
She told me about her baby that was on the way

She seemed so helpless and full of despair
I think all she needed was someone to care

I looked for a way to show her God's Son
But the register rang my order was done

I wanted to tell her it would be all right
But I picked up my coffee and drove out of sight

So I pray for her now that she gets what she needs
And I wished I had planted a better seed

Few Months Ago

I saw a woman I met a few months ago
She was happy for sure it really did show

She showed me a picture of a baby so dear
It was clear to me; God had taken away her fear

Her husband has been working his job did not end
God gave them the money they needed to spend

She asked about my son and me
I could feel her concern it was plain to see

I told her I was working and busy all day
I told her about our Easter play

She told me she would like to come to our show
The seed I planted has started to grow

A Parents Prayer

I love you Lord and I know you care
I thank you Lord for hearing my prayer

Please keep my children safe and sound
I fear they are lost and need to be found

Their hearts and mind seem so far away
Their enticed by the world and want to play

They go out at night and I'm not sure why
Then I can't sleep so I pray and cry

Please hear my prayer from my heart
And give my child a brand new start

Let them feel the love
That comes from above

I thank you lord that the battle is won
Because of Christ, your only Son

Now I must share with you something I have been carrying around in my heart for years. My brother in law that I knew for only a short time was sick with cancer. During this time I spent with him he asked Jesus to come into his heart and to forgive him of his sins. He was a good man and took care of his family, but he knew he must prepare for the end of his life.

It says in the word of God **Hebrews 9:27** And as it is appointed unto men once to die, but after this the judgement.

The last day he was with us on this earth, he was in much pain in body and mind knowing he would soon leave us. I went into his room to see him and he took hold of me by the arm. He had a hold of me so tight that he was hurting me. He said they had to do surgery on me today without anesthesia so I could be here tonight to say good bye to everyone. He said I cried out to God in my agony and pain and the angles came and took me to a beautiful garden and cared for me. They told me I would not suffer much more that it was almost time for me to go. He said it is such a beautiful place, I saw trees and plants more beautiful than anything I have ever seen. Then he made me promise to tell his family and others about Jesus. Here's the hard part, he said that a lot of them were not going to make it into Heaven because they don't know Jesus as their personal Saviour.

Everyone of us must come to the place in our own heart, mind and soul to realize our need for forgiveness of sin in our life. You need to be looking for him.

Hebrews 9:28 So Christ was once offered to bear the sins of many; and unto them that look for him shall he appear the second time without sin unto salvation.

John 3:36 He that believeth on the Son hath everlasting life: and he that believeth not the Son shall not see life; but the wrath of God abideth on him.

Heavenly Insight is in memory of him.

Heavenly Insight

As I prayed to the Lord in the early morning light
He started showing me things that were hidden
from my sight

He showed me heaven with its streets of gold
And how much fun it will be to meet the saints of old

The crown of righteousness he will give to me
The most beautiful robe you ever did see

The sky and the lakes were such a dark blue
He showed me the tree of life and said that's for you too

At the marriage supper of the Lamb when
we're with God's Son
Giving him thanks for all he has done

Suddenly tears flowed heavy, great tears of despair
As I realized some of you will not be there

I dropped to my knees and called out to God above
For my sons and daughter and the family I love

That they would find the redeemer God's only Son
To receive forgiveness for all they have done

I prayed for the people I see every day
Even the ones who won't listen to what I have to say

That they would unlock their hearts and drop to their knees
And give their life to Jesus the one with the keys

LIFE SORROWS

Ecclesiastes 3:1-2 To every thing there is a season, and a time to every purpose under the heaven: A time to be born, and a time to die; a time to plant, and a time to pluck up that which is planted;

Ecclesiastes 3:4 A time to weep, and a time to laugh; a time to break down, and a time to build up;

Valleys of Despair

I've been going through the valleys of deep despair
Searching for the answers here and there

Looking everywhere for peace of mind
Looking for answers of any kind

People will ask you, how is it going?
Yet walk away without knowing

Is there one that understands my troubles and fears?
Do you know the one that can dry all my tears?

There's a heaviness down deep inside
It threatens my existence I fear I could die

Not knowing the truth that would release my soul
Not understanding how to be made whole

Can you show me how to be free from sin?
Can you show me how to have peace within?

Will you take me to that place where peace resides?
Will you go with me there will you kneel by my side

Philippians 4:7-9 And the peace of God, which passeth all understanding, shall keep your hearts and minds through Christ Jesus. Finally, brethren, whatsoever things are true, whatsoever things are honest, whatsoever things are just, whatsoever things are pure, whatsoever things are lovely, whatsoever things are of good report; if there be any virtue, and if there be any praise, think on these things. Those things, which ye have both learned, and received, and heard, and seen in me, do: and the God of peace shall be with you.

A Bad Day

When the Doctors say there is no hope
When you find yourself at the end of your rope

When your Boss tells you today is your last day
When you call home searching for the right words to say

When everything around you seems to turn upside down
When you feel so weak you can't even frown

When you feel lonely, and full of despair
Just turn to Jesus He's always there

You will find Him in your darkest night
He will lead you to safety and into the light

The love and comfort that only he can give
Will fill your heart with peace and the desire to live

He's prepared a place with streets of gold
Thank God his hand is there for me to hold

Psalms 118:8 It is better to trust in the Lord than to put confidence in man.

Divorce

We argue and fight almost every night
We yell and scream what a pitiful sight

Our words are harsh they're meant to hurt
Later I'm sad I feel lower than dirt

There's no winner when it comes to divorce
When the wheels of justice turn, they take their course

Divorce is not a thing to choose
All involved are going to loose

Now I sit at home all alone
Hoping for the ring of the phone

I look at the world it looks like a game
Many of my friends are ending up the same

I feel so lost and ashamed
I try to find someone to blame

I feel hopeless and full of despair
Is there anyone that really cares?

I thought I knew why I wanted to leave her
But I was fooled by the master Deceiver

At the time I knew nothing about God's love so dear
I was lost in my sorrows and full of fear

Now I know who's behind my jealousy and hate
Too bad I found out a little too late

Now I cling to Jesus, God's only Son
He's healing my heart of what has been done

Ezekiel 11:19-20 And I will give them one heart, and I will put a new spirit within you; and I will take the stony heart out of their flesh, and will give them an heart of flesh: That they may walk in my statutes, and keep mine ordinances, and do them: and they shall be my people, and I will be their God.

I Prayed To Our Lord

I heard about your son whose life has ended
So I prayed for your family that your hearts
would be mended

I prayed to our Lord, I began to seek
I searched for an answer but could only weep

I prayed for peace and comfort that only God can give
I asked our Lord why he could not live

He said the place I prepared was ready for him
So I opened the door and I let him come in

I am moved to tears when I think of your sorrow
We never know what may happen tomorrow

But our Lord is faithful to take us through
For God's love and ours is sent to you

1st John 4:16-17 And we have known and believed the love that God hath to us. God is love; and he that dwelleth in love dwelleth in God, and God in him. Herein is our love made perfect, that we may have boldness in the day of judgment: because as he is, so are we in this world.

Things to Remember

The love and courage she showed us every day of her life
The dedication to family as mother and wife

The steps taken together hand in hand
As we walked in God's path and master plan

The times we faced hardships that made us cry
The times we looked eye to eye

The joy and laughter she brought to us all
Will be one of the things missed most of all

The way she was always willing to share
The way her heart showed how much she cared

So many good things about her have not been told
She left us with memories only our heart can hold

Proverbs 31:10-12 Who can find a virtuous woman? for her price is far above rubies. The heart of her husband doth safely trust in her, so that he shall have no need of spoil. She will do him good and not evil all the days of her life.

In Memory Of Philomena Coy
My Mother-In-Law

She is a mother, a friend someone dear
When someone so special leaves, we shed a tear

She was full of love and always smiled
We all prayed that she could stay awhile

Her kindness and love were an example to all
To all in the family whether big or small

She raised six children forming the thoughts of their mind
She raised them to be loving and kind

Six more like her and herself makes seven
God looked down one day and took her to heaven

The Friend I Lost

I saw this man everyday
He had become quiet with not much to say

He had retreated to a place only he knew where
A place he seemed not willing to share

It was a place that tormented his troubled mind
It gave him no rest of any kind

He chose to leave friends, family and wife
I am so regretful he took his own life

If only he knew the peace only God can give
To make the right choice and choose to live

I met brother Dugan in December 1999. A few years later we were involved in a revival of ten area churches. A lot of planning went into this. What I remember most were the prayer meetings we held at the churches involved in the revival. He always greeted me with a smile and had time to spend with me. I valued him as a true brother in the Lord. I know I will see him again one day.

In Memory of Brother Dugan

He was a man that always had a smile
He was a man who would listen and talk awhile

He was a man who always had time to care
He was a man who was always willing to share

He was a man who was always loving and kind
A better man would be hard to find

He knew it was more Blessed to give than Receive
He Preached the Gospel so we would believe

He will be missed by his family young and old
He filled us with memories only our hearts can hold

He was a man of Faith he's only gone for awhile
On Resurrection Day we will all see his smile

THE FINAL DAY

Matthew 24:36-39 *But of that day and hour knoweth no man, no, not the angels of heaven, but my Father only. But as the days of No-e were so shall also the coming of the Son of man be. For as in the days that were before the flood they were eating and drinking, marrying and giving in marriage, until the day that No-e entered into the ark, And knew not until the flood came, and took them all away; so shall also the coming of the Son of man be.*

A Dangerous World

We see terror and destruction caused by men's evil intent
Designed by the hearts of men whose souls are hell bent

We hear of storms of great magnitude as never before
Hearts of men failing them, not knowing what
life has in store

We see a world that seems to be reeling out of control
By forces men search the stars and the earth to know

Suddenly the earth kicks up her feet like an angry child
Heaving up and down causing oceans to go wild

A furry released from deep within
Could it be God's judgment on a world full of sin?

We see death and destruction such awful despair
Is God checking the hearts of men to see if they care?

His anger released on nations gone astray
Unregenerated hearts of men going there own way

Men living out their lives making their own path
That can only end up in the presence of God's wrath

One word, one gesture by God's holy hand
Changes the course of man and his plans

He holds the blueprint for all of man kind
It's his will we must search with our hearts to find

Jesus is Coming is a poem I wrote many years ago. I know everything I write is given to me by the inspiration of the Holy Spirit. I can always apply scripture to verify the messages given to me. Jesus is coming back.

Act 1:6-11 When they therefore were come together, they asked of him, saying, Lord, wilt thou at this time restore again the kingdom to Israel? And he said unto them, It is not for you to know the times or the seasons, which the Father hath put in his own power.

But ye shall receive power, after that the Holy Ghost is come upon you; and ye shall be witnesses unto me both in Jerusalem, and in all Judea, and in Samaria, and unto the uttermost part of the earth. And when he had spoken these things while they beheld, he was taken up; and a cloud received him out of their sight. And while they looked steadfastly toward heaven as he went up, behold, two men stood by them in white apparel; Which also said, Ye men of Galilee, why stand ye gazing up into heaven? this same Jesus, which is taken up from you into heaven, shall so come in like manner as ye have seen him go into heaven.

Jesus is coming back to establish his kingdom. World events right now are lining up and scripture is being fulfilled daily.

II Thessalonians 2:1-12 Now we beseech you, brethren, by the coming of our Lord Jesus Christ, and by our gathering together unto him, That ye be not soon shaken in mind, or be troubled, neither by spirit, nor by word, nor by letter as from us, as that the day of Christ is at hand. Let no man deceive you by any means: for that day shall not come, except there come a falling away first, and that man of sin be revealed, the son of perdition; Who opposeth and exalteth himself above all that is called God, or that is worshipped; so that he as God sitteth in the temple of God, shewing himself that he is God. Remember ye not, that, when I was yet with you, I told you these things?

And now ye know what withholdeth that he might be revealed in his time. For the mystery of iniquity doth already work: only he who now letteth will let, until he be taken out of the way. And then shall that Wicked be revealed, whom the Lord shall consume with the spirit of his mouth, and shall destroy with the brightness of his coming:

Even him, whose coming is after the working of Satan with all power and signs and lying wonders, And with all deceivableness of unrighteousness in them that perish; because they received not the love of the truth, that they might be saved. And for this cause God shall send them strong delusion, that they should believe a lie: That they all might be damned who believed not the truth, but had pleasure in unrighteousness.

This man will arise to power. He will be very charismatic. The whole world will worship him.

Revelation 13:8 An all that dwell upon the earth shall worship him, whose names are not written in the book of life of the Lamb slain from the foundation of the world.

Revelation 13:15-17 And he had power to give life unto the image of the beast, that the image of the beast should both speak, and cause that as many as would not worship the image of the beast should be killed. And he causeth all, both small and great, rich and poor, free and bond, to receive a mark in their right hand, or in their foreheads: And that no man might buy or sell, save he that had the mark, or the name of the beast, or the number of his name.

We are on the threshold of change. People in every nation are looking for someone to solve the economic collapse of our now called Global Community. We are getting accustomed to hearing phrases like, the World Banking System. Our nations around the world are working together in search of an answer to economic confusion and the end to terrorism and war. But the answer is only found in the word of God.

Psalms 118:8-9 It is better to trust in the Lord than to put confidence in man. It is better to trust in the Lord than to put confidence in princes.

The apostle John was allowed to see and record the end of this world system. He saw the Heavens open up.

Revelations 19:11-16 And I saw heaven opened, and behold a white horse; and he that sat upon him was called Faithful and True, and in righteousness he doth judge and make war. His eyes were as a flame of fire, and on his head were many crowns; and he had a name written, that no man knew, but he himself. And he was clothed with a vesture dipped in blood: and his name is called The Word of God. And the armies which were in heaven followed him upon white horses, clothed in fine linen, white and clean. And out of his mouth goeth a sharp sword, that with it he should smite the nations: and he shall rule them with a rod of iron: and he treadeth the winepress of the fierceness and wrath of Almighty God. And he hath on his vesture and on his thigh a name written, KING OF KINGS, AND LORD OF LORDS.

The events taking place around the world are the birth pangs before the return of Jesus.

GET READY JESUS IS COMING

Jesus Is Coming

Jesus is coming and you're not going
If the sins of your life are still showing

He shed his blood to cover them all
But you need to heed his call

You say I'm a good person he would not do this to me
If you don't open your eyes you will one day see

There will be a world leader in charge of it all
You won't have a choice but to heed his call

He will give you a mark so you can work, buy and sell
But if you take it you're going to Hell

People tried to tell you before it was to late
That God the Father has set the date

God will send a strong delusion to all non believers
Now your leaders the Master Deceiver

He will treat you nice for three and a half years
Then he will fill all your worst fears

At this time God will pour out his wrath
On all the people that took the wrong path

What Do You Know

I could tell you of things you've never been told
I could tell you the things that are neither, bought or sold

I could tell you things about the days of old
I could tell you about Paul who spoke so bold

I could tell you about the Holy Ghost and fire
I could tell you about my hearts desire

I could tell you about my troubles and fears
I could tell you things that will bring you to tears

I could tell you about the evil that's all over our land
It numbers, so high as the grains of sand

I could tell you things you've never heard
I could tell you things that sound absurd

I could tell you things you would not believe
I could tell you about Jesus whom you need to receive

I could tell you of things that are dear to me
I could tell you things you need to see

I could tell you God's truth he's told me so
I could tell you things you need to know

So I pray to God that you will one day hear
Because the end of this age is very near

Message From Above

There was a man who came, a longtime ago
He had a message for the world and seeds to sow

His message gave hope it began to grow
He had knowledge from the Father we needed to know

The people followed him everywhere he went
They knew he was the promise, The Father had sent

He healed the sick and the broken hearted
It is in our heart a work has started

He gave us a promise of the Holy Spirit
We must get on our knees and pray to hear it

He will open the secrets of his word
He will tell us things we never heard

All the world leaders and all their guns
Cannot compare with God's only Son

For he's the peacemaker for all who believe
For all who love him for all who receive

He's the hope for all of mankind
He's the truth that you need to find

John 14:6 Jesus saith unto him, *I am the way, the truth, and the life: no man cometh unto the Father, but by me.*

Terror In America
911

Terror and evil has touched our land
And people everywhere give a helping hand

Many people are full of fear
And for the ones we have lost we shed a tear

When the next day dawns we ask god why
And we look with fear at the clear blue sky

Many people realize our world is in trouble
So they run back to church and attendance is double

They cry out to God and say, why was this done
But many don't know God or his Son

So they look to our leaders and military might
And they think peace and safety is in their sight

But I'm telling you now you need Jesus in your heart
When you ask him in you'll have a new start

Only then will you see how blind you once were
A peace from within will begin to stir

You'll see that God is in control
And when it is over he will reach his goal

Isaiah 59:8 The way of peace they know not; and there is no judgment in their goings: they have made them crooked paths: whosoever goeth therein shall not know peace.

Terror Continues
November 2, 2001

Terror by day terror by night
There seems to be no hope insight

Anthrax has been found, in our mail
Every day it's the same old tale

We look at the news every day
Hoping that someone has found a way

To stop this and all the threats
I know Satan's behind it, that's a sure bet

As the days of Noah it shall be
When the coming of our lord we will see

Some think it's not time for our lord to come
He will take those who are looking but leave behind some

So don't be caught unaware
Troubled by the world and all its cares

Because Jesus is coming for you and for me
And every knee shall bow and every eye shall see

A Cry For Peace
911

The peace of our land has been threatened
Many fear this war could lead to Armageddon

Our tears should flow, our cheeks be wet
As we pray to God to have our needs met

Please forgive us Father for what we have done
And we thank you Father for the gift of your Son

We need to pray for our nation on bended knees
And ask God for peace that we long to see

But all of our planes fly out of their hangers
We strike back with bombs and with righteous anger

For to innocent people this evil deed has been done
But only on our knees will the battle be won

God has a message for all that will hear it
But you can't know it without his spirit

So ask Jesus in
A new life begin

And with the peace of god you will know
That the spirit of God runs the show

The Final Day

When the final day has come
When that last souls been won

The Father will say to his Son
Go get your bride the hearts you've won

Those that love you and believe
Those that hear you and receive

Gather them up from here and there
Bring them to me the one that cares

The tears they shed they'll shed no more
Show them the promises I have in store

For those whose hearts are filled with my love
The love of my Son that was sent from above

Matthew 24:30-31 *And then shall appear the sign of the Son of man in heaven: and then shall all the tribes of the earth mourn, and they shall see the Son of man coming in the clouds of heaven with power and great glory. And he shall send his angels with a great sound of a trumpet, and they shall gather together his elect from the four winds, from one end of heaven to the other.*

I was at work today and I was praising God singing songs and praying for my family, the pastor of our church asking God to move in a mighty way in all our lives. The spirit came over me and I began to weep while running my machine. I thought about what I had been praying for with tears still filling my eyes, I stopped running my machine and stood at my tool box listening to what the Holy Spirit had to say.

Talking About You

Jesus is weeping, weeping for you
His heart is broken almost in two

He was crying so hard I felt his hurt and sorrow
Of what could happen as soon as tomorrow

I received a message of how it could be
Now say to yourself is he talking about me

This Could Be You

I heard about God's precious gift
But I continued to be lost and adrift

I didn't believe he'd come back so soon
And now I fear I am doomed

I cry out to God and say, where is my mother
My father, sister and even my brother

Where is my daughter and my son?
Oh my God what have I done?

My aunts, uncles and my cousins
Their all gone more than a dozen

I ran to the church to see what has happened
But there was no one there singing and clapping

I should have listened while there was hope
But as usual I acted just like a dope

I scoffed and laughed at God's Son
Now I am lost because Jesus has come

I should have listened to God's word
But I closed my ears and never heard

Now I hope you can see how it will be
When the children of God you no longer see

But his spirits still here listen while you can
Because God has a master plan

Open you heart, mind and soul
Give him your heart which Satan has stole

Jesus gave his life to set you free
So heavens gates you will one day see

With tears of joy he'll let you in
And eternal life you will begin

Romans 6:23 For the wages of sin is death; but the gift of God is eternal life through Jesus Christ our Lord.

1 John 5:11-12 And this is the record, that God hath given to us eternal life, and this life is in his Son. He that hath the Son of God hath life; and he that hath not the Son of God hath not life.

1 John 1:9 If we confess our sins, he is faithful and just to forgive us our sins, and to cleanse us from all unrighteousness.

COME TO HIM WHILE THERE IS STILL TIME

DECISION TIME

This is not the end, but only the beginning. I have filled this book with many scriptures.

Psalms 119:130 says The entrance of thy words giveth light; it giveth understanding unto the simple. And in **Psalms 119:160** Thy word is true from the beginning: and every one of thy righteous judgments endureth forever.(Forever) That is why I say it is decision time. This can be your day to enter into the promises of Eternal Life being restored to your rightful position as a child of God, or as John tells us Sons of God.

John 1:12 But as many as received him, to them gave he power to become the sons of God, even to them that believe on his name. You need to receive him and believe on his name and you have been given the power to do this.

Why Do I need to do this?

Romans 6:23 For the wages of sin is death; but the gift of God is eternal life through Jesus Christ our Lord. Paul is talking to all of mankind.

Romans 5:8 God commendeth his love toward us, in that, while we were yet sinners, Christ died for us.

John 3:17-18 For God sent not his Son into the world to condemn the world; but that the world through him might be saved.
He that believeth on him is not condemned: but he that believeth not is condemned already, because he hath not believed in the name of the only begotten Son of God.

Romans 10:9-10 That if thou shalt confess with thy mouth the Lord Jesus, and shalt believe in thine heart that God hath raised him from the dead, thou shalt be saved.
For with the heart man believeth unto righteousness; and with the mouth confession is made unto salvation.

Romans 10:13 For whosoever shall call upon the name of the Lord shall be saved.

Are you ready to call on his name? Just say this simple prayer.

Dear Heavenly Father, today I confess to you that I am a sinner and I receive your Son's sacrifice on the cross for my sins. I believe and receive your forgiveness and love provided by your Son Jesus Christ. I receive him as my personal Saviour. I know that you raised him from the dead and he sits at your right side and one day where he is I will be also. With my whole heart I confess Jesus is my Lord and Saviour.

This is the first step in your new life in Christ, now find yourself a Bible believing church and fill yourself with his word.

Printed in the United States
214418BV00001B/2/P